Fun
and Games
in Marriage

Fun
and Games
in Marriage

Dorothy T. Samuel

Word Books, Publisher

Waco, Texas

... *We can somehow endure pain, provided we can grasp a loving hand and be supported by a familiar arm. We can live through failure if only one dear companion goes on believing in us. But what we cannot endure is the experience of being utterly alone, without anyone to love us or care about us* ...

—David R. Mace in
   Marriage As Vocation

Contents

Foreword

THE INVITATION to write a Foreword to Dorothy Samuel's book brings me both pleasure and pride—pleasure, because I like very much what she has written; pride, because our association has been such that I can detect, in these pages, refined and polished, a few ideas I have shared with her. Dorothy's husband, Will, was once a graduate student of mine. Then, years later, they both shared with my wife and myself two training experiences in marriage enrichment. So I know not only Dorothy and Will, but also Dorothy-Will as a deeply happy and united couple.

What I am saying is that the author of this book is writing with the authority and authenticity of personal experience of marriage as vocation and as relationship-in-depth. But of course there is no need for me to say this; any discerning reader will become aware of it at once as he peruses these pages. There is a freshness in her approach that stands out in sharp contrast to the dreary claptrap and hollow cynicism that too often characterize the talk about marriage that abounds these days on the printed page, the stage, and the screen.

Dorothy sent me, as she began to write, her first efforts, and asked me for my candid opinion. I saw in them the promise of more and better things to come and encouraged her to go on working at her material. She has done so with diligence, and as I now read her finished manuscript I know that she has a rare skill with words. She knows how to choose them felicitously, and to weave them into bright and beautiful patterns, pleasing alike to the eye and to the ear. This is a gift, but it does not come without effort. "Genius," said someone, "is industry polished till it shines." I'm not sure that I believe that—about genius. But I do know that a well-written book must be polished till it shines; and this is that kind of book.

What we have here, however, is much more than well-chosen words. Enshrined in the words are penetrating and arresting and challenging thoughts. And again and again the thoughts and the words blend, like musical instruments in perfect harmony, to stir and awaken us to new awareness, as though we heard again, in an unexpected moment of sweet surprise, a haunting melody long forgotten. For Dorothy Samuel is not telling us something new; she is recalling to our failing memories truths that are old and ageless.

She writes vividly about the subtle overtones and undertones of married love which our dulled perceptions have ceased to hear, or which we have dismissed as too commonplace to be worthy of our notice. Then suddenly, as we read, it all comes alive to us; and we see that beauty and joy are to be found not in the goals we so feverishly pursue, but in the daily litany of life itself, the thousand little acts of kindness and of love that so often go unnoticed or unremembered.

This is a book about marriage; but it is a very unusual book about marriage. It is a paean of praise for married love, sounded at a time when married love is more often spoken of with cynicism and scorn. It is a book to read and re-read, a book to give to a spouse or to a married son or daughter or friend. It is a book to keep handy; indeed, for any married couple it is the perfect "bedside book," in both senses of that ambiguous term. I congratulate the author, and commend cordially to the reader what she has written for our enjoyment.

DAVID R. MACE

Life's
Little Bumps

Chapter 1

Life's
Little Bumps

It is seldom the great tragedies that wreck a marriage. If a couple have anything at all going for them, they rise to the demands of sudden job loss, death in the family, serious illness. Indeed, they may often be bound together by facing great problems jointly and sustaining one another.

It is the minor frictions, the petty irritations—annoyances too slight and temporary to justify discussion and compromise—that can kill a marriage. You rush into the bathroom for a late shave, and find wifey washing her hair in the bowl. You finally squeeze out an hour to trim your pet rose bushes, and go out to find hubby soaking them with the hose. You save an afternoon to switch the tires, and find wifey has lent the car to her brother for the day. You have scrubbed the floor painstakingly, and come back with wax and cloth after it is dry to find hubby has the malfunctioning electric percolator parts spread out for a repair job. Like so many mosquito bites, these exasperations produce a constant aggravating rawness; stung by the annoyances, the disposition is scratched to an accelerating ache by the tension of withholding comment and retaliation.

No couple can avoid these irritations; any two persons sharing one house will get in each other's way from time to time. The closer and more intimate the association, the greater the opportunities for stumbling over each other and each other's peccadillos.

So enjoy it! Don't squeeze by each other in the narrow passageway—bump into each other! Make passing as difficult as possible, extending rumps and elbows, jostling shoulders and hips. Exploit every opportunity for "fun and games" and the delicious sexual stimulation of the passing rub and the sensuous pressure.

Daisy is rushing supper, heading for the sink with a hot hard-boiled egg to be water-cooled. But Abner decides just then to fill the watering can. A potential bickering session? A "Must you do it *now?*" and "I'm only trying to take care of *your* roses" strain on togetherness? Not necessarily. Daisy pushes herself against Abner, exaggerates a provocative "You're in my way," rubs shoulders, exchanges a sparkling glance, lengthens thigh against thigh —and maybe even maneuvers the egg under the water above Abner's sprinkling can. Or perhaps the egg becomes lost in the ensuing fun and games. The fun and games make marriage a joy for life; eggs last but a mealtime.

Any psychologist can see the therapeutic values of this, of course. The possibility of conflict is deliberately used as an invitation to love play. Exaggeration of an annoyance relieves the inner tension even as it signals a much more delightful substitute activity. And this is good. But it is negative only, turning kitchen sex play into a creative form of conflict resolution.

Kitchen sex play, dear married couples, is a positive good!

It needs no therapy justification. Indulged in for itself, it is a great marriage stimulator and one fine way of saying "I love you."

Most of the time we *can* pass each other in the front hall with ease. But why do it? The passageway has brought us together and provided a great opportunity for walking directly into each other, breast to breast and thigh to thigh. And those little two-person chores—hanging curtains, putting up pictures, storing away storm windows . . . Why hold something out before you when, by holding it to the side, your arm can rest its way along your spouse's back or chest or waist? Why stand to the side-to place bread on the table when you can reach around your spouse's neck and feel a beloved head nuzzle into your side?

Shaw once said that "marriage combines the maximum of temptation with the maximum of opportunity." Too many marriages lose the "maximum temptation" as soon as the first excitement of sexual exploration is over. But we are sexual beings; our whole marriage structure grows out of this enjoyment of the flesh. We must not let the merchandisers of sex narrow our joys to the short moments of actual intercourse. To do this brings us to today's cliché: having sex more and enjoying it less. Intercourse that represents nothing and culminates nothing becomes a pretty routine experience. The joy of the bed is fed by a multitude of little joys and excitements which run through the days, making it fun for two people just to be together.

Wondering about those earlier illustrations? Well, I once heard of a husband who scooped soapsuds off his wife's head for a fragrant shaving lather—and she had a lot of fun before she finally got her hair in shape two hours later. I saw a work-shorts-clad wife walk right into the stream of hubby's hose before she deflected it back at him, and two drenched characters later shared a crowded tub to clean off each other's dirt. The percolator—well, sometimes we have to compromise. But compromise is not nearly so hard when, most of the time, we fall over each other at every opportunity.

There's a charming little parable of the new bride who had prepared muffins to surprise her husband. Just as she smelled them beginning to burn, the young husband called excitedly from the back porch, "Hurry, darling! You must see this sunset before the last light goes!"

How do you finish the scenario? "But my muffins . . ." and a burnt finger and two minutes later, the bride meets the husband coming in dully. "It's too late now." Mutual disappointment, hidden resentments, no spirit to appreciate muffins anyway? Or do you see a quick run from the scorching smell, arms entwined on the back porch, heads close in the mystery of a night's beauty, followed by hilarity over the truly burnt offering when they come in together from the shared moment?

Choose ye this day whether yours will be a muffin marriage—orderly, practical, businesslike, and dull; or a sunset marriage—inspiring, exciting, loving, and slightly fey. Muffins are eaten and forgotten; the entwining of souls lasts and grows.

I Love You

Chapter 2

I Love You

In the hills of Vermont, where words are not wasted and emotions not expressed, a taciturn couple in their eighties rocked silently one night on the porch as had been their custom all the years of their marriage. Painfully, speech finally burst from the old man.

"Sometimes, Mandy," he muttered, "I love you so much it's almost more than I can do not to tell you."

Most of us are not Vermonters. We don't like hypocrisy, either, and we know fine words are no substitute for action. But we know also that action may spring from many motives—duty, habit, martyrdom, as well as love. And most of us are not really very secure or self-confident deep inside. We all have times of despondency and of feeling alone and unloved. A mate who frequently reassures us verbally that we are loved can make flowers of joy spring up everywhere.

There are so many other things we tell each other:

You upset Mrs. Jones again this morning with your flippancy . . .
You don't make the children mind . . .

21

You'd always rather break something than read the instruc-
tions . . .
You're wearing the brown tie with the blue shirt again . . .
You left the butter out again . . .
You jinx every machine you touch . . .

If we can bear to repeat these complaints over and over
again, why can we not bear to repeat those time-worn
words "I love you"?

"I love you." It's commitment and invitation and comfort and support and cheer and medicine. However abused
one may feel in the midst of the pressures and frustrations
of a busy day, those words come as a sudden balm. The
exchange of glances, the quick touch, the immediate response in kind—perhaps no more can be squeezed in at the
moment, but the tasks suddenly are easy, and the heart
is happy.

Many a husband has felt the weight of an employer's
disapproval and his own sense of inadequacy melt as his
wife cries "I love you" and embraces him at the door. He
is someone again, someone important and treasured and
understood.

There is no better way to interrupt a busy spouse, when
interrupt we must, than with a fond "I love you." Pref-
aced by that atmosphere, the call we must make upon
service or energy comes into a receptive ear. There is no
more reassuring remark after a party with charming people
than "I love you." So often the very presence of other
charming people of the opposite sex makes us intensely
aware of how blessed we are to be married to our own
unique specimen. But our own unique specimen may not
always be so sure—unless we say it.

A refugee in Germany after the war found herself utterly bewildered by the loving service Friends rendered in their non-evangelical way. At last she asked why, and the American Friends Service Committee worker explained to her Friends' vision of the God in every man and the brotherhood which makes all men objects of our love. Greatly touched, the refugee burst out, "But, my dear, you must preach what you practice!" There is a lesson here for every couple.

Speaking and doing are two sides of a single coin. Only the word clarifies beyond doubt the great mystery of love's motivation behind the acts that make life smooth. Only the word carries the constant reminder in the doldrums of mundane activity; only the word sings in the ear and repeats itself in the memory.

"I love you" when there is sadness, and "I love you" in moments of joy. "I love you" when one senses the other needs support, and "I love you" when one feels need for reassurance oneself. Even "I love you"—a bit ironically perhaps—when exasperated.

And with the words come the actions and the reactions, rippling on and on, cause wrapping tail around effect, until every moment is saturated with that one incontestable fact of marital existence: I love you; I am loved.

Publish
Glad Tidings

Chapter 3

Publish
Glad Tidings

ONE OF THE WAYS our spouse hears "I love you" is as it rebounds from others who form the setting of our married lives. He reads it in their faces and hears it in their voices; he feels it in the squeeze they give his hand and recognizes it in the almost envious respect they show him—if we have been loving him in their presence.

All that we say or do concerning our spouse comes back into his life. "I love you" can come back to him through the people we see and live among. For it is not only quite obviously possible for any married person to wreck the reputation of his or her spouse through the tales told and the comments dropped; it is also inevitable that our sense of joy in our marriage partner will communicate itself to relatives, friends, and associates.

The wife who shares only the delightful things her husband does, who speaks of him with loving joy, who obviously misses him when he must be away, is building a picture of her husband as a man who is really a success— a success in the most demanding interpersonal relationship of all. A husband who speaks of his wife with deep affection, who tells of her wise decisions and kindly actions,

who is openly grateful for her help and respectful of her
judgment, is telegraphing "I love you" to her through every
person he meets.

We do not all do this. Even happily married people often
fall into the trap of indulging in sex-stereotype jokes and
put-downs. Many a husband who really does consider his
wife a good driver just can't resist the temptation to mock
her publicly. For the sake of a male-group joke, he makes
her a cliché. He may think she'll understand, and, in a way,
she does—she understands that he is a poor, weak little boy,
more interested in publishing his masculinity than in telegraphing love. The wife who really appreciates her husband's help in the kitchen may still crack wise about his
clumsiness or ignorance or mess-making—not because it is
true, but because she prefers publicizing her female supe-
riority to telegraphing love. She makes her husband a joke,
a thing to be laughed at.

And our moments of disappointment, pain and sorrow?
Well, it is in sharing these that a spouse offers us the greatest strength and love. It is in meeting these jointly that
marriage most deepens and grows. If my husband has hurt
me, it is my husband who should learn my feelings and my
husband with whom I should seek a way to avoid future
hurts. Time enough to talk to outsiders when I can report,
instead of the hurt, the magnificent way in which my husband enabled us to face a difficulty and go forward with
new understanding. Then I shall be telegraphing love.

For our mate's dirty linen should be as out of sight as
our own, and eventually laundered as thoroughly as our
own. We do not go around telling demeaning stories about
ourselves. Even when we admit some act of which we are

not proud, our confession is largely composed of the reasons, the extenuating circumstances, the basic goodness in ourselves revealed by this very admission that one particular act was not in keeping with our fine principles and usual sterling conduct. This is an instinctive manifestation of our natural self-love.

In the same manner, we love our spouse—protecting his name, publicizing his virtues, explaining when surface appearances are confusing, and believing firmly in his underlying principles and conduct. We publish our love in the stories we tell and the jokes we make. Those who run may read, and the message is loud and clear: here is a person able to make one other person fully love and trust him.

Whenever those who have received such a message from us meet our mate, their attitude is a message from us to that mate: I love you.

Maintain
Maximum
Temptation

Chapter 4

Maintain
Maximum
Temptation

The swingers—the group sex middle-class marrieds—
like "their fellow Americans, have now gone from
Puritanism into promiscuity without passing
through sensuality."

—critic Molly Haskell in *The Village Voice*

Marriage should be that middle way. It should be that
human relationship in which the joys of the flesh, the development of the sense of touch, and the evocation of physical joy peak within a context of real love and mutual
concern. There really is no other state which can offer
an exultation in the physical apart from exploitation and
selfish satisfaction.

Therefore appearance—which is the invitation to full
exploration—does play its part in married joy. After we
have disqualified all the cheap substitutes—the lecherous
girl-watchers on the street and the strip teasers in the night-
clubs; after we have acquiesced to youth's insistence that
the clothing is not the person; we are still left with the raw
fact that the *same* person can look either delightful or de-
pressing. The same person can provide Shaw's "maximum

temptation" or turn the other person off with a carelessness of dress and flesh and carriage that seems to shout "I don't give a damn about you." And this is as true of those who lean toward the cut-offs and sweat-shirt uniform as of those who hold to the nylon hose and shirt-and-tie uniform. It is not the style of dress, not the formality or informality, that makes one person a joy to behold and another dull or even repellent.

The good cook proudly affirms that she bakes her pies and sets her table to delight her husband. Shall I be ashamed to say that I choose my clothes to delight my husband? That I keep my figure to delight my husband? Is the appetite for a taste thrill somehow more genteel than the appetite for a touch thrill? Two who would be one seek to delight each other in all ways at all times. And the sanction marriage provides for the sensual gives the physical thrill a peculiar importance, for it is special to the twosome in a way that a good dinner or a magnificent painting or a symphony concert can never be.

We marry because we want to be wanted; we build beautiful marriages when we continue to be the kind of person our mate will want. And while no amount of physical beauty can compensate for spiritual poverty or emotional clutter or intellectual barrenness, the fullest union between fine characters has a mortar of the physical. That mortar is not beauty, but brightness and vivacity and cleanliness and the appealing disposition of the flesh under clothing and without clothing.

The young are right; it is not clothes that make the man. But clothes are a reflection of the body that lives beneath them; they may provide variations and moods and subtleties, and they may enhance sensual joy. So may clean shining hair and firm, erect bodies; taut flesh and laughing eyes.

Marriages are constantly recharged when one mate's appearance in the room—even in the kitchen for breakfast —excites a gleam of pleasure and downright physical appreciation in the eyes of the other. Marriages are constantly recharged when one mate's appearance in the room elicits in the other a desire to touch, to bump sensuously in passing, to remember and anticipate the joys of the private night. That tingle of good, wholesome sensuality keeps marriage vital when each maintains "the body electric" and rejoices in it for the sense of health it gives and the pleasure it brings one's mate.

Two
Shall Be One

Chapter 5

Two
Shall Be One

ONE FLESH, one heart, one mind—one house, one room, one bed, one bedtime. Psychiatrists are writing much these days of the sexual cop-outs of middle-aged married people. One study found that late-night TV shows provide excellent rationale for an avoidance of sex. Confirmation of this conclusion was provided amusingly when the breakdown of a coaxial cable left one town in West Virginia without TV for a short period of time. Nine months later, the birth rate tripled. What is good for the birth control promoters may not be good for the quality of marriage.

Togetherness is a spiritual quality, but like any other spiritual quality, it is developed and sustained by regular practices. Character isn't built in sudden crises, and the love that makes one + one = ONE is not built by sudden copulation. To coin an epigram, the more you share, the more you share; anything which contributes to the life apart contributes to the life apart.

The double bed requires some adjustments. Light sleepers marry hit-the-pillow sleepers; restless dreamers marry dead-weight types; morning people marry night people.

What fun! Just as couples fit themselves into the physical
curves and angles of each other's bodies for copulation, so
couples can curve themselves into the patterns of each
other's personalities. And the union that comes in so doing
is far more cohesive than the union of occasional physical
penetration.

To know another's body and movements so intimately
that each moves in harmony with the other as a waltz
partner—this is marriage. To lie down together at the end
of a day, to stretch however briefly against the loved one
while the physical tensions flee before the soft glory of
flesh pressed to flesh; to lie in the dark and share the usually
unspoken thoughts, the apologies and compliments each has
repressed, the secret dreams and the precious visions—this
is marriage. To cap these with a prayer, a shared moment of togetherness in the great ecology of the universe,
is to build self into self inextricably as the roots of two
sturdy trees mesh the ground of their being. For such,
sleep itself becomes a form of intercourse.

Maximum temptation plays here its part also, and frequently the sharing flows into the physical before sleep—
a natural extension of a spiritual exploration, and a great
physical symbol of an inexpressible dearness on all levels
of communication. Sexual passion of this abiding and enduring sort is not available by appointment nor readily
expressed when a mate must be called from another bed,
another room, another activity.

"The two shall become one," the Bible promises. But
not just in moments of orgasmic linkage do two become one.
Rather, because two are becoming one, orgasmic linkage
becomes a tender reality—a physical manifestation of an

intangible unity which permeates all the moments of life.*

It is, therefore, the creation of opportunities for that spiritual union which we must carefully nurture. Techniques of intercourse cannot create love where love is lacking, but love creates its own techniques of intercourse magnificently relevant and joyous to an already united couple. Intercourse supersedes in ecstasy the rut of barnyard animals precisely as it expresses something more than the physical response of male to female. The more it has to express, to symbolize, to embody, the more joyous it becomes.

And so, not only double beds but double lives—in the same sense of the word—go into the building of a truly happy, satisfying, and enduring marriage. No longer have most of us the old farm family framework where the work, the problems, the plans, the needs, the joys and the successes of husband were interwoven with those of wife. The separations enforced upon most of us by the very distance of work from home, the specialization of the information and skills required to earn a living, the ensuing screening of hurts and failures of a working day from the spouse require of us *more* conscious care in sharing, communicating, growing together.

There are, of course, no rules. Careers vary in their demands as personalities do in their responses. But a marriage built upon the guiding principle that all growing experiences that can be shared shall be shared is a marriage

---

*Science provides confirmation. "Lee Rainmaker . . . found that among white couples in which wives shared some activities with their husbands, 64% greatly enjoyed sex. Only 18% of those who did not share other activities with their mates reported such enjoyment of intercourse." *Psychology Today,* July, 1971, p. 99.

in which two people will grow closer and grow together toward the same goals as life progresses.

Religious experiences, for instance, should be shared. A successful partnership can be built on mutual tolerance as each goes his own way; an entwining of two spirits as one cannot be. Religion is a broad term. Not only the obvious worship forms should be shared, but also concerts which lift the spirits, lectures which open new horizons for the mind, books which touch the springs of personal morality or dedication. All should be shared—physically shared. For most people, these are largely off-the-job enrichments. It is worth great sacrifice in time, money, and effort for couples to attend mind-stretching programs together. Better for the marriage two great surges of growth a year—shared—than a dozen captured hit-or-miss by one or the other.

A great deal is written of the undereducated wife who cannot keep up intellectually with her executive husband. Too little is recognized of the greater disparity (not sex-linked) which more frequently reduces a marriage to a business deal—one partner growing and glowing in leaps of the spirit while the other stays on the spiritual level of the wedding day. It happens so easily; one remains behind to "make muffins," or to save money, or to loaf before TV, or even most nobly to make all the excitement possible for the other. This latter is no self-sacrifice; it is marriage-sacrifice and self-deception. Anything from which great joy, inspiration, renewal, stirring is expected, should be shared: the quiet week in the woods, the seminar on relating to today's children, the retreat led by an inspirational writer, the ecology panel, the craft camp. From these we often return different people, feeling the need to make basic changes in our life style. Such "conversion" experiences can be conversions of the *we*, not the *I*. These moments of sudden insight or change of direction can be so thoroughly shared that subsequent growing pains from adapting life's decisions to increased wisdom become mutual exercises in discovery and implementation and support.

There will be enough unexpected, solitary experiences. By rushing home like school children to pour them out before they lose their freshness, these experiences can be incorporated into the marriage that is already firmly built together. Couples sometimes forget, over a period of time, to which one a particular experience actually occurred, so completely has it become woven into "their" experience.

It is the same with jobs, specialized or not. When I married my husband, chemistry was about as far from my interests as anything could be—much further than the activities of my job were removed from his understanding. But I was interested in him, completely interested. As more than eight hours of his day, six days a week, revolved around chemistry, I became very interested in the activities and problems of an industrial chemist. This was not a put-on, a pretense, a good-wife bag. Nothing interested me more than he—his thoughts, ideas, laughs, and sorrows; as so many of these involved the chemical work, that work was truly interesting as a part of him.

This sharing adds luster to every homecoming; it makes possible envisioning the other while away. In our own lives, it made possible really mutual consideration and decision at the time when my husband began to think of a complete change of profession. I could never have performed his job, but there was nothing really important about the values and decisions and people involved that I had not come to know and appreciate intimately. Change of vocation was, therefore, truly *our* decision.

"Marriage is vocation," David Mace promises. For those who see it as that area in which success is most important, all other things become a part of this main goal. All other decisions are made in the light of the primary question: how will this affect our marriage? For some couples, jobs must be changed because they do not allow for the ultimate togetherness; for some, location must be changed; for almost all, some habits and pastimes and even friends must be relinquished in order to allow time for the shared experiences which really bind two individuals together.

And for all, the shared room and the shared bed at the shared bedtime restitch the fabric of shared life which imparts a kind of holiness to the shared flesh. If marriage be our vocation in life, nothing short of illness, death, or emergency should keep us from this nightly lying down together. All else—transient pleasures, opportunities, interests—are mere muffins in the oven.

Bring the Girl/Boy-Friend Home

Chapter 6

Bring the
Girl/Boy-
Friend Home

SHARED LIVES not only bring joy; they prevent sorrow, misunderstanding, suspicion, and complication. A wife who hears eagerly the details of her husband's work, the problems posed by relationships with his co-workers, the excitement of conferences or meetings after hours, is not likely to dream up nonexistent "other women" or groundless fears that her husband is overeager for opportunities to spend time away from home. She participates emotionally in every encounter, eagerly sending him forth, and excitedly awaiting his return to learn how "their" plan worked out.

His work, *her* dream—these are the old "feminine mystique-y" pronouns. Today, many a husband has an attractive, able, wage-earning wife who spends eight hours a day in the company of other males who deal with her as a woman and as a human being. Suspicions about her reactions to male associates whom she mentions regularly may be as much a problem to such a husband as the old, imagined "other woman" was to the housebound wife. And sometimes both husband and wife allow their imaginations to build threats until one or the other is psychologically pushed into prophecy fulfillment. It is all so unnecessary. That veil of mystery can be torn aside. If these outside associates are interesting enough to play any real part in the life of one of the spouses—a personal, friendly part— they are interesting enough to be incorporated into the building of a one + one = ONE marriage.

Indeed, they must be. For almost worse than the unvoiced suspicions about the male or female often mentioned by a partner is the separate-lives solution. Those couples who try to sell themselves on some kind of "new morality" to provide a rationale or ethic by which to endure the unendurable are most miserable of all. Any counselor can affirm how often the proudest exponents of these advanced moralities of sexual freedom and marital independence are covering up for a sense of humiliation they reveal only in the most confidential intimacy. One can have total marriage union, or one can have just a business relationship under the title of marriage, but one cannot mix the two without great pain. The half world of partial self-giving and partial isolation—with its ever-changing lines of demarcation—is a real hell. No ego survives it intact.

So, wives, bring your male friends home. Husbands, invite that interesting woman you work with to lunch— when you're meeting your wife. Enjoy these people! But share the enjoyment—the fun of discovery and relationship development. Make each of them "our friend," so that the experiences and satisfactions and discussions are shared pleasures of husband and wife. Like shared books, shared friends enrich the marriage relationship.

And shared friends are real friends. Those who are truly on our wave-length will find an exchange with Bob-plus-Mary to be far richer than an exchange with either Bob or Mary cut off from half of his or her whole self. Such friends come to think of us as a couple, to talk of us and to us as a couple even when only half the couple is physically present. They come to treasure us for that special richness found only in a personality comprising both masculine and feminine elements.

But nothing must ever be said to a friend in the physical absence of one's mate which would not have been said in his or her presence. A friend is not a person to whom one runs with tales and from whom one expects sympathy for the little irritations one hides from one's mate. A friend is one with whom one shares one's joys and sorrows, yes; but if the "one" doing the sharing is a one + one = ONE, it is the joys and sorrows of the ONE that are shared. In so doing, the ONE bind becomes stronger; the very presence of the friend enhances the marriage. And having no secret vent for irritations encourages each partner to learn that there can be no secrets in a happy marriage; either an irritation really is too petty to be spoken—in which case it is too petty to allow oneself to feel—or its very emotional importance requires that the marriage gain the rich experience of facing and handling the irritation honestly.

Is this not, quite apart from the sex of the friend, one of the basic reasons for jealousy of a mate's associates? As long as the lives of a husband and wife are compartmentalized into "my" friends and "your" friends, there is a nagging fear that "your" friends are being told things that would

make me unhappy, are learning of my weaknesses and im-
perfections and failures, are bolstering "your" side of any
story of our problems.

Bringing the boyfriends and girlfriends home early in the
association transforms them into "our" friends. It is possible
to have every friend be a strengthening of the marriage,
another shared pleasure tying two people together. A friend
who is reacting to Bob-and-Mary, who thinks of Bob as a
couple and Mary as a couple, reflects back that oneness.

One of the very nicest introductions my husband and I
ever received was when a young man pulled another up
to us and told him: I want you to meet one of my best
friends, Dottie and Will Samuel. May all marriages provoke
such confused grammar!

I Got There First

Chapter 7

I Got There
First

Marriage is always. That is its glory, of course, but it is also its point of vulnerability. Always. Through the blahs, the headaches, the periods of overwork, the emotional pressures of parents, children, neighbors, the spilt milk, and the perversity of machines, marriage takes no vacation.

Before marriage, when you felt like biting everyone's head off, you canceled your date. When you had gas pains that made moving uncomfortable, you stayed home and took it out on mama. When every single thing that could go wrong had gone wrong—your lipstick broke, the dog chewed your last pair of hose, your father used up the hot water, your sister "borrowed" the blouse you planned to wear, your mother ordered you to do the dishes before leaving—at least, you turned to your arriving date as to an angel coming to whisk you away from a world of injustice and cruelty. If anything, you found yourself more loving because here stood the one "innocent" in a world of selfish, mean, and infuriating people.

But marriage is forever. And when the coffee boils over and the baby wets your lap and the last bottle smashes on the floor and the bulb burns out and mother calls to remind you that you promised to write Aunt Mabel this very evening—it's hubby who is on the scene, possibly making his own demands.

He may just have found his last clean shirt missing a button, wet diapers lying on his magazine, an important letter unmailed in his coat pocket, and a new wisdom tooth aching its way through his gum.

No knight in shining innocence to whirl you away from an uncaring universe now, he appears as the author of your problems. And, in turn, he glares, not at a beautiful young vision who can transport him from his own mundane world, but at a woman who has loaded him with responsibilities while seeming to shirk her own. But one word, just one word of complaint from either partner, and the gripes become accusations become recriminations become hurts and wounds and cruelties never to be unsaid.

Now, some people claim to like these sessions. The ecstasy of release, akin to the stoning of witches in an older day, brings on a kind of blood lust which culminates, eventually, in a wrestling match on the bed. This form of sex, hardly to be called "play," exhausts the adrenalin and is euphemistically described as the "fun of making up." The mate becomes a sort of beloved adversary for awhile —an emotional punching bag which offers back a kind of chiropractic massage, invigorating, challenging, and sensual. For awhile.

Perversely perhaps, but none the less psychologically true, the wild passion of such rut on the bed is rapidly forgotten; the angry words, the selfish demands, the unfeeling accusations remain in the memory. The following day is far more likely to find each reliving the battle than the orgasm; meditating on sharp answers that might have been made rather than anticipating another night in bed. Over months and years, the wounds fester, and the memories feed upon each other, until each ego is humiliated, and trust has fled. Which words are really meant—the passionate words of love or the equally passionate words of scorn and anger? In time, neither the speaker *nor* the hearer is any longer sure which words represent the true feeling.

Yet these times of "I can't take any more" do come. If marriage be vocation, such times of stress can become opportunities to grow in love, understanding, and communication.

Suppose a great disaster. However tired you might be, if your mate fell off a ladder and broke a few bones, you would forget your own physical and psychological pains instantly to rush to aid, to comfort, to care. With a broken body at the foot of the ladder, as with all really serious disturbances of one partner, that partner comes first! As long as that need is great, the other partner simply puts aside his or her own little problems.

In a good marriage, a marriage forever, the same overriding concern for the other and for the ultimate endurance of the marital relationship exists in lesser crises. A half-joking recognition of this—only *half*-joking—can enable couples to meet the much more frequent little horrors as well as they instinctively meet major disaster. Because qualitative weighing of need is impossible in life's little crises, a simple "first come, first served" forms an equitable basis of choice.

"Don't you blow up now—I got here first!"

Seldom will it be said quite so crassly, but the principle is sound. Some couples communicate so openly that a wife on the verge of tears or a husband about to swear can say honestly: "Everything went wrong today; I've got a headache and sore feet; my disposition is foul. Don't push me right now."

And it has happened in our own home, occasionally, that I was about to say the same thing! But if he "got there first," he is the one who fell off the ladder for the moment. My own aches must become ways of empathizing. For the marriage is the important thing—not my disposition; the marriage is forever, and my temper changes a dozen times a day.

Not always are things so openly phrased. Indeed, the more serious the emotional disturbance, the less likely it is to be put so clearly. But when two people love each other, the first irritable response is a signal. If a loving wife snaps at a perfectly natural request from her husband, he can recognize a need for a little extra consideration as clearly as if she lay injured at his feet. He tables his request, and offers to do something to lighten her load at the moment; he shows affection a bit more obviously; he puts himself out to understand; he creates a healing atmosphere of peace and good nature and love.

In the little things! Oh, those little things. When the wife who would usually note, "Gosh, we forgot the garbage again this morning," accuses instead, "*You* didn't put the garbage out *again!*" it is no time for defensiveness. Even if it would be absolute truth to respond, "But you said not to bother because you didn't have to leave till 10 this morning," a husband who puts the marriage first will not say it. He will recognize the sign; his wife fell off the ladder first. "I'll do it right now," is a sufficient response. And he follows up with other help and a bit of extra loving until she's rested her feet and regained her normal disposition. It won't be long; love responds to love surely and gratefully . . . and ever more quickly in a marriage where each is willing to put the health of the marriage ahead of the momentary satisfactions of blowing off. And each is more able to do this when it is clearly recognized that his own turn is coming—that "first come, first served" is the principle of selection, not some unfair role assignment by which one or the other must always be the mature, understanding, self-controlled spouse.

Interestingly enough, this kind of response pattern has a way of culminating in the bed, too. But these are orgasms from the ecstasy of going deeper and deeper into unity, not the passion of battling each other into a physical blend. Sex, after irritation has been used as an opportunity to express love, has something very wonderful to express.

You Never Listen to Me

Chapter 8

You Never
Listen to Me

Tom Lehar caustically expressed a frustration many of us feel with people who are always complaining that they can't communicate: "If people can't communicate, the least they can do is shut up about it!" Better, I suggest, that they "shut up" and let others communicate with them.

Anyone who has ever watched two young people in the totally abstracted state of first, ecstatic love has observed the secret of real communication. Each has eyes only for the other. The boy may be reeling off the most boring set of baseball statistics, but the girl's eyes never leave his face. She is listening with every fiber of her being because she wants to know everything about him—from the things which absorb him to all the inner personality which lies beneath the actual words. The girl may merely be describing her difficulty in choosing between two dresses, but the boy's eyes search every flash of expression, and his ears are eager for the music of her voice. Both may become real nuisances to other friends with constant "Tom said this" and "Mary said that" reminiscences.

Something happens after marriage. It is rather like the

way we visit the historic landmarks of our own city only when we're entertaining out-of-town guests. Because we can go any time, we never get around to going at all. Because we can listen to our mate any time, we may never get around to listening at all.

Some people handle this problem with extended separations, finding that the moment of return revives the old undivided attention. Unfortunately, the practice also tends to develop an increased ability to enjoy separation and to live without any communication at all.

Far better a date with one's own wife—a quiet place, a served dinner, and just the two, one husband and one wife. If people have anything at all to share and to talk about, a dinner table with no kitchen duties, no telephone, no doorbell, no work waiting in the next room, and no children near brings it out. Follow dinner with a ride into the country—no distractions again, and an opportunity for a little provocative snuggling, a little hand-on-the-knee affection, while exchanging those unexciting anecdotes and experiences and dreams that the pressures of living have pushed off for some "better time." Spend the night at a motel. A quiet room together where the phone cannot ring, a guest cannot drop in, unfinished work cannot tempt, is a wonderful setting for real listening to each other, sharing with each other, interpenetrating each other spiritually, and— still relaxed and unpressured—sharing sex without the fatigue and rush that so often precedes bedtime at home.

Such dates become more than just an occasional high spot in a dull marriage. The "date" can be an exercise for *communicating without ceasing*. When St. Paul advised Christians to "pray without ceasing," he certainly did not mean for them to spend all their time in a prayer closet, but rather to carry the prayer closet atmosphere over into every other activity of the day. Just so, a couple must devise communication closets in which to grow so close that the atmosphere carries over twenty-four hours a day.

There are fun ways to increase our sensitivity to a mate, to make ourselves better listeners while drawing out of each other a deeper, more intimate and real level of conversation. The first-love couple do these things instinctively; the motel night may revive the instinct. Couples can look at each other! We can look at each other whenever one is speaking—centering our attention, opening our inner selves fully to the other, looking deep within the eyes of the speaking partner for that spirit which can be only partially revealed in mere words.

And we can stop playing guessing games with each other. Embarrassment, fear of misunderstanding, unselfishness— as well as sheer spite—often lead a married person to make only oblique references to something very important to him or her—and then to feel unloved and rejected when the hint is missed. If anything is important enough to feel badly about afterward, it is important enough to state clearly for the mate's consideration.

The wife of a very busy minister once came to feel that he had time for everyone's problems but her own. She had wandered about the house looking hurt, made vague references to "being a little upset," and even dropped a few comments about an area in which she was having trouble making a decision. To no avail. He loved her; he respected her ability to handle problems—and he was constantly being called upon by people who quite openly told him they needed his help. This was the typical stage setting for a poor marriage: husband absorbed in important work which he felt his wife also cared about deeply; wife choosing between building a separate world of her own or lapsing into self-pity and nagging. She found a third alternative. She called him on the phone and told him quite frankly, "I'm deeply disturbed about a choice I have to make involving my whole future, and I need spiritual counsel. Could I have an appointment with you this week?" A time was set; the problem she had been wrestling with was clearly described; they discussed it seriously and at length; the final decision was a joint decision. And they were immeasurably closer for the sharing.

It should not be necessary to go through married life making appointments with one's mate, but such appointment may be the finger exercise by which we learn to play a symphony of full, constant communication.

$$$$$$$$$

Chapter 9

$$$$$ $$$$

IT IS ALMOST impossible to make money into a fun and games thing. Money just isn't a fun thing! That which money buys can be fun; the mere spending of money can sometimes be fun; the giving of money can be fun. But money itself simply has no tactile appeal, no taste appeal, no smell appeal, no visual appeal. It is a barren thing, as readily symbolizing evil as good.

The only time I can remember feeling a pulse of genuine ecstasy in connection with money was the day my husband and I dethroned it. Deciding one truly could not serve God and money, we knocked the money monkey off our backs. From then on, it became like the garbage can or toilet bowl —indispensable to a pleasant home, but stuck out of sight and never considered in making important decisions.

Not everyone is going to adopt this philosophy. The important thing in marriage is less what philosophy a couple adopts than that they come to a single philosophy. Money is the root of so many troubles because people just don't like to put into words the philosophy they are really living. Therefore, financial decisions are always fuzzy, often contradictory, and sometimes downright dishonest. Marriage simply cannot thrive where there is suspicion of dishonesty, even if there is no intentional dishonesty.

A passionate young man once wrote his sweetheart a letter.

> I love you more than life itself. I would
> climb the highest mountain, swim the deepest
> sea, walk through fire, ice or hurricane
> just to be by your side.   p.s. I'll be over
> Friday evening if it doesn't rain.

The contrast between profession and reality strikes us as hilarious in a joke about someone unreal. But daily, husbands say to their wives, "I love you more than anything in the world, and your happiness means more to me than my own life. But we can't buy the piano which is your dearest creative outlet because we have to increase our savings account." Wives say to husbands, "I love you so much, and I'd do anything at all to make you happy. But you mustn't take that fellowship because we have to store up a few thousand in the bank before risking our income."

These are not people who really can't afford a partner's heart's desire—people who will literally starve or sicken because of an expense. People who *do* have enough income to purchase a real heart's desire often do not hear themselves actually saying what amounts to "I'll come over Friday evening if it doesn't rain." But the mate hears just that, and suspects dishonesty, hypocrisy, empty verbiage of love.

If bank accounts and insurance policies and stocks are prime in a couple's dream of a secure marriage, they must be prime to both—openly, verbally, deliberately prime. A shared philosophy of financial accumulation can then be part of the cement that unites one to the other. Those bank accounts, however, must never be an unexamined "but" that underlies a different philosophy openly, verbally, and deliberately proclaimed.

Couples can dance around any attitude toward money once it becomes *their* attitude. But the lead does not belong with the partner for whom the philosophy is easier. If Daisy's desire for a piano conflicts with the couple's agreed-upon security plans, Daisy must be the one to make that immediate application. This is the time for Abner to offer to breach their philosophy. If saving is truly a mutual phi-losophy, Daisy will revert to it after she has fully enjoyed the moment of delight in Abner's great offer of love. *She* will say the "no, not now." And if saving is not truly a mutual philosophy, the sooner they labor out a mutual phi-losophy, the better.

Later, when there is real agreement that Daisy's piano is a spiritual necessity that can now be afforded, it is better for Abner to be the moving force in actually spending the money. One never "lets" a spouse buy something impor-tant; one insists that the spouse buy it! The long-desired electric saw, the sailboat, the wall-to-wall carpeting—when the money is there, the partner less enamored of the pur-chase can press for action and so add a descant of personal love to the happy song of possession.

It may be harder to believe that it is often best for the less qualified spouse to handle the accounts. In many mar-riages, the poorer manager, the poorer bookkeeper, the poorer arithmetician should pay the bills and balance the checkbook and make the savings deposits and order the magazines and fuel and license renewals. All that drudge work is much more likely to become a "we" thing, and the money philosophy of the couple is much more likely to become a building block in adding one + one into ONE, if the spouse for whom financial responsibility is more difficult is constantly concerned with the details.

Maybe second best always does "try harder." Certainly the actual paying of bills and seeing the balance dwindle is more likely to result in "second best" turning off lights and comparison shopping and controlling impulse than is a constant nag of "we're spending too much" from the practical spouse. All these chores can become a part of the joy of building a marriage; nagging tears the fabric of marriage apart.

There is a positive benefit, too—a real plus to the daily joys and spirits of a couple—when the spouse who is deeply concerned about financial security does not have his nose pushed into it all the time. For most couples, there are periods when the money just is not enough to fulfill their own philosophy of security, whatever that may be. The spouse more deeply dedicated to that philosophy will find his spirits crushed, his self-image shaken, and his confidence eroded every time he apportions an insufficient pay check, reduces the bank balance, or pays another bill. His congealed spirit dims the whole marital radiance, sucks the joy from little pleasures, brings irritation into the simplest exchanges of love.

If doing the dull work of bookkeeping can save a spouse from that constant reminder of inadequacy, how joyous a duty it can be for the more carefree spouse. And how joyous a thing it can be in the marriage, for the marriage is built on the sheer joy of being together, the little laughs and warm glances and dropped kisses which we indulge only when our hearts are light and gay.

For us all, in a sense, money must be a trash can or a toilet bowl. Some will want many toilets, lavishly designed, but none will want them dominating the living rooms of their lives. The joys, the excitements, the intermingling of two people into one whole—these go on in the living rooms of our marriage.

The Marriage-Centered Home

Chapter 10

The Marriage-
Centered Home

THOSE LITTLE cherubs who are supposed to "bring us together" and "cement a marriage" also provide much static
on the wave length of couple communication. *How do you
find time to talk together when there are children?* is perhaps the most frequently asked question at marriage enrichment seminars. The answer, of course: it isn't easy.
And even the motel weekend ploy won't solve this one
unless the motel weekend carries over into day-by-day
communicating.

One of the best pieces of advice I ever received early in
our raising of four active children paid surprising dividends
in marriage enrichment as well as being remarkably effective in bending the little twigs. Take a deep breath; set
aside all old preconceptions (prejudices) and culturally
indoctrinated unexamined assumptions: *the only way to
raise an unselfish child is for the parents to be just a little
bit selfish.*

This applies to many things, from not always offering
the child the last piece of cake to not always letting the
child into the conversation. And the advice is only a corol-

lary of an even more fundamental principle of child-rearing: the greatest benefit one can give a growing child is to
be a happy marriage.

Couple communication—real communication—requires
privacy. Spiritual aspirations, hard financial choices, deli-
cate discussion of sex practices, and real sharing about the
children's development—none of these can be accomplished
with a toddler running in and out or a junior high schooler
asking riddles. Yet these intimate communications are the
very stuff of entwining lives.

Activate the bedroom door and archaic ideas of personal
privacy. When mommy and daddy go into their private
room and shut the door, it should be understood that nothing but fire, flood, or sudden death warrants interruption.
A fan whirring or a radio tuned low will provide enough
background scramble to discourage incipient eaves-drop-
perism.

This is not as difficult a policy to inaugurate as it may
seem, for one teaches more by example than by precept.
Children, too, deserve privacy, and parents who intend to
remain people while being parents will make people of their
children. Once infancy is passed, a child should also have
the right to close his door and know that it will not be
opened without a knock. While children are very small,
that knock may have to be merely announcement for physical safety's sake. But when they grow beyond danger to
themselves or siblings, the knock should be a genuine request for admission—a request which can be denied. Children, too, need space to be alone or to share secrets with a
chosen brother, sister, or friend. To gain this privacy they
will gladly grant privacy to their parents.

The greatest advantage of the closable door, however, does not come from its use in moments of unexpected stress. Regularly, nightly, parents can make use of the private room for a coming together of mind and spirit which alone can make the continuing coming together of bodies meaningful.

When the necessary demands of the day are done, small children put to bed and older children perhaps reading or playing or watching TV in the public rooms, a couple can go off into that private room and take time to unwind together—a soft embrace, relaxed and unobserved; the little chores of undressing together; perhaps a book or pamphlet to read aloud. The physical bodies unwind, and the personal unities strengthen. Then two people can slip into bed in a leisurely, happy—often silly—togetherness. Bed then becomes an unpressured stretching side by side, flesh against flesh, in pleasant but undemanding warmth. Perhaps the bed light is still on; the joys of the simple sharing of undressing and couple-talk hover. And deep communication can begin, there in the quiet haven of the bed, without pressures, without anxiety, and inviolable. It is the daily exercise of the motel weekend special.

Problems that are tackled in this atmosphere become truly joint problems, lovingly shared. Visions that are revealed become couple glories, weaving together the deep aspirations of two hearts. Play that develops then, whether the nonsensical repartee that keeps youth alive or the slowly deepening play of hands on bodies, becomes an outer symbol of such total union as recompenses all daily struggle. And prayer that comes then is a Communion beyond all form.

This is marriage *with* children, rather than marriage *to* children. As with all truly right ways of living, it provides the richest benefits to all—to the children as well as to the parents, and thus to the whole family unit as a little outpost of the kingdom of God on this scarred earth.

In-Laws
in Love

Chapter 11

In-Laws
in Love

THERE WOULD NEVER have been need for the command-
ment "Honor thy father and thy mother" if it came as
naturally as breathing. And if we have trouble with our
own father and mother, no wonder the trouble with a
mate's father and mother proliferates all those jokes. So
what *does* love demand?

As the best training a couple can give their own offspring
is to *be* a happy marriage, the best reward a couple can give
their parents is to *be* a happy marriage. Parents really take
pride in that—and feel all their efforts were worthwhile.
Over years, that glow of pride far outweighs the petty
annoyances and dissatisfactions with a son's or daughter's
choice of spouse.

When a couple has embraced an unconventional decision,
and an in-law is tornadoing about, an in-couple joke or two
helps both the marriage and the in-law situation. The tight
embrace of mutual agreement, the slightly smug shiver of
marital rightness, and the good-humored laugh at the tran-
sience of the moment's storm spell love from the center out.

"Just imagine how mom'll brag about her child-rearing

when we're still happy while her friends' children are getting divorced!"

"One day, dad's going to lay all our success to the way he inculcated independence in me at an early age!"

Love is really a pretty tough thing—and a truthful thing. If two people are really going to become ONE, the sooner everybody realizes it, the better. That "I do" means a man is no longer momma's darling Bobby; he is, hopefully, her loved Bobby-Mary. "I do" means Mary is no longer a daughter rushing home for support, but a Mary-Bob coming home to talk. The sudden transition may be hard for parents, but not nearly so hard as feeling, ten years later, that they reared a weak, dependent, and miserable human being who could not succeed as a marriage partner.

Parents, too, must be woven into the oneness of a happy marriage—the best and the worst of those parents. Neither wife nor husband should be fragmented by conflicting loyalties and obligations to spouse and parents. Rather the couple as a ONE should share totally both the joys and sorrows related to all four parents. There is the early sharing of childhood anecdotes through which the spouse's parents take on character and personality. There is the deliberate sharing of problem areas and difficult personality traits and special needs of one parent or another. And there is the sharing of attitudes and values by which a couple begins to build a single personality and a single set of principles for human relationships.

And there is the fun of exercising that single personality.

"Your mother wants us to come for dinner," one calls from the phone. "What shall I tell her?"

"Whatever you think best."

But—

"My mother wants us to come for dinner. What shall I tell her?"

"I really don't want to get all dressed up again and go out tonight. Can we put it off till Friday—or invite them here Friday?"

The single personality is mutually developed, but in any given problem situation, it is better that it be articulated and activated by the spouse likely to be more reluctant. To visit Bob's parents when a couple has planned an evening at home can be love-building and marriage-cementing—if Mary puts the decision into words. Happy marriages are not built by one pushing the other to live up to the ONE's best, but by each allowing the other opportunities to display the ONE's best.

The most difficult parents-in-law, of course, are those who are unhappy in their own lives. They not only load heavier demands on their sons and daughters, but those sons and daughters are constrained by pity from acting as full human beings. Every couple can decide, however, not to repeat the in-laws' mistake.

For there is, of course, the other side of the in-law problem. Just about the time we have learned to live really easily with the in-laws we married, our children bring us a new set. Then the marital joy and oneness we have built over the years becomes our greatest gift to them—example and inspiration and freedom to a new ONE being created. We leave these young in-laws free not only for their own happiness, but because we have a life of our own—often a greater thrill in the ONE than we've ever had time for before. And what a great gift to adult children not to feel always that mom and dad are miserable if left alone, empty if not living vicariously through them.

The empty nest is a delightfully spacious abode for couples who have been building into each other all the years of their marriage. The fun of leaving the house together whenever impulse strikes, the sensual joy of climbing into a private tub together, the activation of mutual interests and hobbies and causes long relegated to low priority, the blessed quiet, the absence of those little daily demands children in the home make upon time and attention—these are glories of the empty nest. Not even the honeymoon compares to it!

So don't respond to every demand, don't call over every day, don't baby-sit every time. As children-in-law, don't respond to every demand either, don't report every activity, don't discuss every decision. A truly happy couple living a full and interesting life *together* cannot help but spill over love upon in-laws on either side of the age scale; they will have too much love to contain.

Speak Truth
to Love

Chapter 12

Speak Truth
to Love

"This dress really was a mistake, wasn't it? I should never wear this color."

"It certainly dims your natural radiance."

That's truth, not lack of tact.

"I was right to tell her she didn't belong in any school system, wasn't I?"

"No, darling, you were not right to say that to Mary's teacher."

"But you know I only wanted to straighten the situation out."

"Yes, I do know you only wanted to straighten the situation out. But you asked me if I agreed with the way you did it."

That's truth, not carping criticism.

"I feel everyone is being *too* cheerful! Tell me —did the doctor really say it wasn't malignant?"

"No, dear, he didn't. The doctor really said . . ."

That's truth, not cruelty.

Where else is one going to find truth but in marriage? Battered between the meaningless compliments of polite society and the brutal nastinesses of bad temper, demanding bosses, and jealous associates, where is one to find truth?

Where is one to find another human being who so fully respects and trusts our character as to refuse to play games with it, to manipulate it, to prevent it from growing? For even the kindest "protection" assumes we are not strong enough to bear truth, we are not wise enough to make some decision, we are not great enough to grow from facing reality. Where can we be both completely known and completely trusted—except in marriage?

Society tries to throw us off. "Oh, I wouldn't tell Charles that—it would hurt him so." "I can't let Alice know about this—she would worry." Drip, drip, drip—sentimental pap of noble martyrdom and generous duplicity, the foundation of a thousand soap operas where soft little saps tear each other apart with doubts and suspicions and poorly disguised lies.

Love is a tough thing, a demanding thing, a power that lifts the lover to the summit of his potentialities, not a blanket that smothers him or her. Do we picture the love of God as some fuzzy good will that protects mankind from hard choices and inner discipline? If we picture an almighty God who yet gives freedom to the bumbling humans he created, should this not tell us something about love? Love says, "You can do it!" and stands by to help; it does not say, "Poor little idiot, don't bother your inferior mind with growing up."

". . . What we cannot endure," David Mace so profoundly says, "is the experience of being utterly alone. . . ." There is no aloneness more complete than the aloneness that engulfs us when we are surrounded by people we cannot trust to tell us the truth! Then, truly, we are stripped before the universe and at the mercy not only of evil, but of the very people manipulating us according to their own benevolent motives.

Marriage is Truth—ultimate, tough, unfailing Truth—cushioned on everlasting arms of love—but always Truth. And as two people become wholly transparent to each other, eliminating all barriers of you-me, they do become one. What is known to one is known to the one + one ONE; and there is no aloneness any more.

Commitment

Chapter 13

Commitment

OUR WESTERN WORLD is in the process of discarding marriage as an institution. Re-examinations of the relationships between the sexes pour over us until it is almost impossible for individuals really to think and evaluate for themselves. Yet one thing is certain: we are entering a society in which marriage will be what a couple decide it should be; society will no longer dictate either legally or morally.

It is dangerous to move from somewhat light-hearted suggestions into the area of passionate convictions and debate. Passion leads people to respond: if she believes *that*, I won't read any of it—or its equally foolish opposite. Yet no light-hearted techniques of living together can help human interrelatedness unless they are expressions of an underlying spirit.

A young poet I know has expressed some of our modern emotional aridity* putting the prime four-letter vulgarism of our age into its proper context—a vulgarism religious printers still do not like actually to spell out.

*Robert Gautier, poem untitled

Je ne peux pas to melt   (I can't)
" " " " to feel   (I can't)
" " " " to talk   (I can't)
" " " " to love   (I can't)
C'est impossible   (Impossible)

Je peux to – – – – (I can)

Marriage *is* to melt, to feel, to talk, to love; anybody can – – – –. Marriage is also to share, to suffer, to endure—and to be shared *with*, suffered *for*, endured. It is, in its finest expressions, to end that rootless loneliness which is the human tragedy. David Mace says, "We can somehow endure pain, provided we can grasp a loving hand and be supported by a familiar arm. We can live through failure if only one dear companion goes on believing in us. But what we cannot endure is the experience of being utterly alone, without anyone to love us or care about us. . . ." Plato expressed it in the myth of the circles, a *rejoining* of what was once a whole. Jules Romains, in his novel *Le dieu des corps*, makes it part of the religious experience. John Fowles, a towering modern, writes most unmodernly in *The Aristos:* "It is this giving without return, this helping without reward, this surplus of pure good, that identifies the uniqueness of man as well as the true nature of the true marriage. This is the quintessence [that] the great alchemy of sex is for; and every adultery adulterates it, every infidelity betrays it, every cruelty clouds it."

The cornerstone of such a marriage is commitment. However one modifies the shabby outer forms, there must be a "till death do us part" in the heart of each partner. We do not always reach our goals, but we never reach a goal we have discarded. Holding a goal informs our every action and reaction with a quality, a color, a flavor that could never be exhibited without the inner goal and dedication. Permanent relationships cannot be built on a "ships that pass in the night" attitude; complete sharing will never be risked when the sharer may become the accuser, ridiculer, even enemy, in the near future.

The evils of Victorian duty and enforced continuance of unendurable marriages came from the application of external force, often to people who had not really chosen each other in the first place. Commitment is a highly personal dedication, freely arrived at, and enforceable only by the person himself or herself. It is as different from legal restrictions as the spirit of worship is from rote observance of a formal church service. It is the only marriage "technique" that is universally applicable and universally effective. It is to know that one person loves you so much—the deep, lonely, essential, inner you—that he or she has committed himself to be a part of you forever *regardless of consequences*, regardless of your superficial frailties and your day-by-day stupidities.

I know of only one easily observed parallel. Unfortunately, the parallel is not obvious to very young people. But any parent knows how many times while children are growing up they go through stages in which they seem completely foreign to all the values, interests, and desires the parent cherishes. At these times, we are tempted to feel—with no animosity toward the child—that it would be better for that child to be in a different family, and for us to be without the day-to-day exacerbation of that child's temperament and personality. But we do not divorce a child!

We work harder, love harder, understand harder, compromise and accommodate harder. We learn how "to melt . . .
to feel . . . to talk . . . to love." And we usually wind up
loving that child forever. With a child, we may never
come to agreement—he may truly have a fundamentally different life set—but we do continue to love and be deeply
interested in him forever.

If we can experience this personal growth and this enrichment of understanding with a child—a child we know
is only lent to us and must develop his own unique nature
—why can we not experience this personal growth and this
enrichment of understanding with a spouse whom we have
freely chosen just because of a deep inner compatibility?
We make a commitment to a child sight unseen, healthy
or crippled, bright or retarded, compatible or wildly un-
like us. We do not divorce a child; we are too keenly aware
that he needs us. We "melt . . . feel . . . talk . . . love"—
and we don't even have a four-letter experience to repay us.

In any love marriage, our partner also needs us. He
has invested something of himself in us; bound his aspirations and emotions, his self-image and his outer reputation,
to us. Commitment carries us through his unpleasant
"stages," and in so doing, enables him to keep growing and
to pass through them.

Commitment not only affects the one making the commitment; it affects the one receiving the commitment. One
does things very differently when he knows his partner is
truly committed. One plans differently for the future, decides vocation differently, looks at producing children differently, handles his own weaknesses differently—one even
has intercourse differently. Marriage becomes different; it

becomes not an institution but an interweaving, not an agreement but an at-one-ment. In time, it becomes not a "we *won't* part," but a "we *can't* part"—for where one begins and the other leaves off is no longer discernible.

There are, of course, no certainties, no inevitable happy endings. I cannot promise: do this and you will have a wonderful marriage. I can say that, without this, you are unlikely to have more than a dully satisfactory marriage. But that is what commitment is all about; it is laying your life on the line for something more valuable to you than any "practical" considerations. It is what the old saints had when they chose "this day" whom they would serve.

Marriage has the possibility of becoming a little outpost of the kingdom of heaven here on earth only when it is *for real*, and it is for real only when it is the expression of a commitment—a commitment as complete and entire as we make to a child we bear.

Date Due

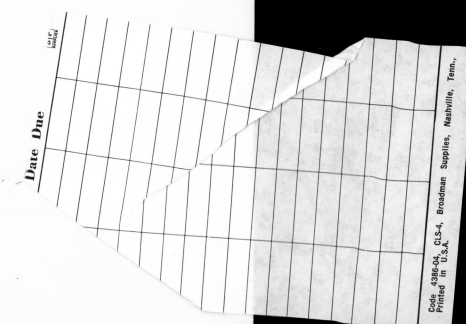

Code 4386-04, CLS-4, Broadman Supplies, Nashville, Tenn.,
Printed in U.S.A.